GETTING TO KNOW THE WORLD'S GREATEST ARTISTS

LEONARDO DA VINCI

WRITTEN AND ILLUSTRATED BY MIKE VENEZIA

Consultant: Sarah Mollman

CHILDREN'S PRESS®

An Imprint of Scholastic Inc.

New York Toronto London Auckland Sydney
Mexico City New Delhi Hong Kong
Danbury, Connecticut

Dedicated To Jeannine

Cover: *The Last Supper*, 1498, Santa Maria delle Grazie, Milan, Italy
© FineArt/Alamy Images

Library of Congress Cataloging-in-Publication Data

Venezia, Mike, author, illustrator.
 Leonardo da Vnci / written and illustrated by Mike Venezia. –
Revised edition.
     pages cm. – (Getting to know the world's greatest artists)
   Summary: "Introduces the reader to the artist Leonardo da Vinci"–
Provided by publisher.
   Audience: 8-9.
   Includes bibliographical references and index.
   ISBN 978-0-531-21312-4 (library binding : alk. paper) – ISBN
978-0-531-21289-9 (pbk. : alk. paper) 1. Leonardo, da Vinci,
1452-1519–Juvenile literature. 2. Artists–Italy–Biography–Juvenile
literature. 3. Scientists–Italy–Biography–Juvenile literature. I.
Title. II. Series: Venezia, Mike. Getting to know the world's greatest
artists.

 N6923.L33V43 2015
 709.2–dc23
 [B]   2014042741

TIMELINE OF LEONARDO DA VINCI'S LIFE

1452 Leonardo is born in Vinci.

1467 Leonardo moves to Florence to become an apprentice in the art studio of Andrea del Verrocchio, one of the best artists in Florence.

1472 At age twenty, Leonardo is accepted into the important Florence Artists Guild.

1475 Michelangelo, another great artist of the Renaissance, is born.

1482 Leonardo moves to Milan to work for the duke of Milan. The duke is eager to use Leonardo's many talents, especially his ideas for designing war machines. Leonardo starts making detailed drawings in what would become his famous notebooks.

1495 Leonardo begins working on a painting for the monastery of Santa Maria delle Grazie. *The Last Supper* would become one of Leonardo's most famous paintings.

THIS WAY

1499 When the French army invades Milan, Leonardo goes to Venice.

1502 Cesare Borgia, a feared military leader, hires Leonardo to be his architect and military engineer.

1503 Leonardo returns to Florence, where he begins painting a large mural, as well as the *Mona Lisa*. He is given permission to dissect human bodies. He makes hundreds of notes to better understand how the human body works.

1513 Leonardo moves to Rome as a guest of the Pope. Two other great artists, Michelangelo and Raphael, are working in Rome at the same time.

1516 Leonardo moves to Amboise, France. There he lives comfortably for the rest of his life, working on his notebooks, science studies, and inventions.

1519 Leonardo da Vinci dies peacefully in Amboise.

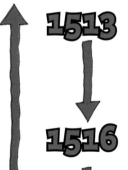
UP HERE

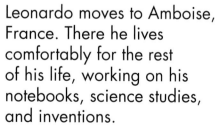

Self-Portrait. 1514.
Drawing.
Biblioteca Reale, Turin.
Art Resource

Leonardo da Vinci was born in the small Italian town of Vinci in 1452. He kept the name of his town for his own last name.

When he was little, Leonardo drew
pictures of plants, insects, flowers,
animals, and birds. He drew what he
saw in the countryside near his
home.

Leonardo da Vinci lived during a

time when people all over Europe were becoming interested in art. They wanted their cities, houses, and churches to be filled with beautiful statues and paintings. This period of time was called the Renaissance.

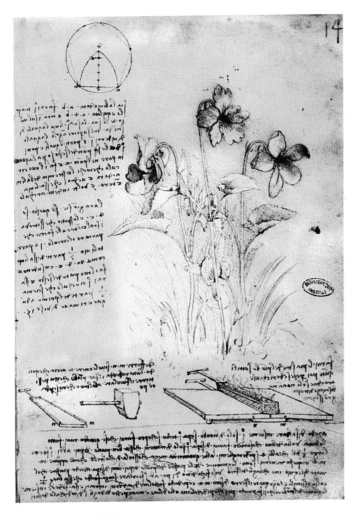

Botanical study. 1505. Drawing.
Bibliothéque de Institut de France, Paris.
Giraudon/Art Resource

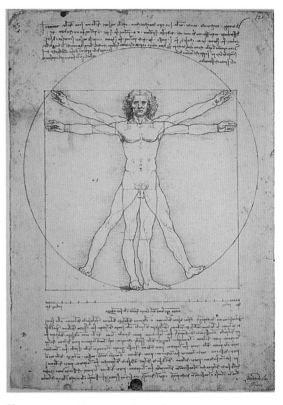

Human proportions reconstructed
according to Vitruvius.
1487-90 Drawing. Accademia, Venice.
Scala/Art Resource

Leonardo was a great artist, but he
became famous because he was able
to do so many other things, too. He
was an architect, a musician,
sculptor, scientist, inventor, and

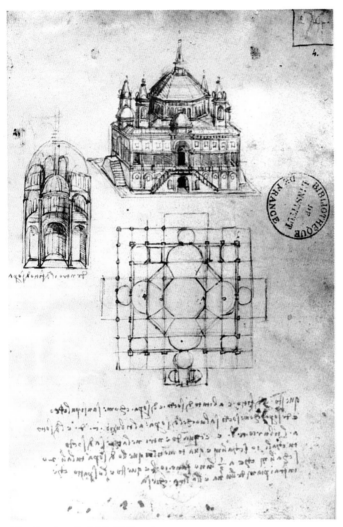

Plan for church. 1487-89 Drawing.
Bibliothéque de Institut de France, Paris
Giraudon/Art Resource

Plan of ideal city.
1487-89 Drawing.
Bibliothéque de Institut de France, Paris
Giraudon/Art Resource

mathematician. Leonardo designed
plans for beautiful churches, bridges,
even whole cities. He used his
drawings to help him see how things
would work.

Leonardo made lots of notes with his drawings. The unusual thing about the notes was, they were all written backwards!

To read Leonardo's notes, you would have to hold them up to a mirror. He probably didn't want people to read about his discoveries or steal his secrets.

The Annunication. 1472. Tempera and oil on wood. Uffizi, Florence. Scala/Art Resource

Leonardo used what he learned
from nature and science to make his
paintings look real.

In this painting, he made the angel
wings from the things he had learned
about bird wings. Leonardo knew
how to paint beautiful plants, trees,
and mountains, too.

When he was a teenager,
Leonardo's father took him to

Baptism of Christ.
Andrea del Verrocchio.
1472. Oil.
Uffizi Gallery, Florence.
Scala/Art Resource

Florence, Italy, to learn about being an artist at the workshop of the famous Andrea del Verrocchio. Florence was one of the greatest art cities in Europe.

When he was twenty years old, Leonardo helped his teacher finish this painting. Leonardo painted the angel kneeling in the lower corner.

Many people in Florence thought Leonardo's angel was the best part of the picture because it looked much more like a living angel than the other stiff-looking figures.

It wasn't long before Leonardo was asked to do whole paintings by himself.

Detail of *Baptism of Christ.*

Ginevra de'Benci. 1474. Oil on wood.
National Gallery of Art, Washington, D.C.

Leonardo painted beautiful portraits. In this picture, he used what he had learned about nature and science to make the background as realistic as the lady. Leonardo made this painting so smooth you can hardly see a brush mark.

La Madonna Benois.
1478.
Oil on wood.
Hermitage Museum,
St. Petersburg.

Leonardo was one of the first
artists to paint the mother of Jesus
smiling and playing with her baby.
Before this, artists showed Jesus and
his mother looking very serious.

St. Jerome. 1481 Underpainting
Vatican Museum, Rome. Scala/Art Resource

The Adoration of the Magi.
1481-82 Underpainting. Uffizi, Florence.
Scala/Art Resource

Leonardo was asked to paint these two pictures, but he never finished them! Nobody knows why. He left other paintings unfinished, too. Maybe he got too busy with his experiments and inventions.

The people of Florence may have heard about Leonardo's unfinished paintings.

About 1482 Leonardo decided to leave Florence and go to another great art city, Milan.

One of the first things Leonardo did when he got to Milan was paint *The Virgin of the Rocks.*

This painting was very important in the history of art. Before it was painted, most artists would outline their people and use very flat backgrounds. Leonardo painted his figures without outlining them.

He made the shadowy part of the people almost blend into the mysterious background. The parts of the people that have light on them seem to come forward and appear almost three-dimensional.

The Virgin of the Rocks. 1506.
Tempera on wood.
National Gallery, London.
Scala/Art Resource

A lot of people must have liked *The Virgin of the Rocks,* because a few years later Leonardo painted another one. They look almost exactly the same.

Look at how much more lifelike Leonardo's painting is than this painting, which was done about the same time by another artist.

Madonna and Child.
Filippino Lippi.
Tempera and oil
   on wood.
Metropolitan Museum
   of Art, New York

War Machine. 1485. Drawing. British Museum, London. Marburg/Art Resource

Before Leonardo moved to Milan, he promised the duke of Milan that he would make him war machines to protect the city against the duke's enemies.

This seemed like an unusual thing for Leonardo to do, because he was a very gentle person who hated war.

Leonardo made lots of drawings of these machines. Some of them seemed as if they would work, but some of them looked like they wouldn't work at all.

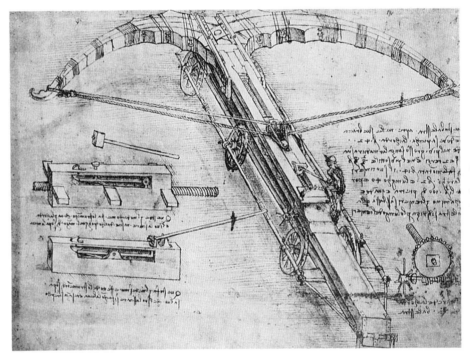

Armored Car.
1485. Drawing.
British Museum, London.
Marburg/Art Resource

Giant Crossbow.
1489-90. Drawing.
Codex Atlanticus, Milan.
Art Resource

21

THE LAST SUPPER

Leonardo da Vinci's greatest work was done for the wall of a dining room that was used by the monks at the Church of Santa Maria delle Grazie, in Milan.

The Last Supper shows Jesus with his closest friends, the twelve apostles.

Leonardo used all the things he had learned while doing his earlier paintings. The shadows, lighting, and background make this a beautiful painting.

The Last Supper. 1495-1497. Fresco. Santa Maria Delle Grazie, Milan. Scala/Art Resource

The special way Leonardo placed
the men around the table gives them
a feeling of movement that had never
been seen before.

Detail of *The Last Supper* (before restoration)

A few years after Leonardo painted *The Last Supper*, the paint began to chip off. Leonardo made his own paint and sometimes it didn't work very well. In the late 1900s, art experts restored the painting. On the cover of this book, you can see how it looks now.

The Last Supper isn't the only painting that gave Leonardo problems. In one painting of a battle scene, the paint almost melted off the wall when Leonardo tried to dry it with fire pots.

The *Madonna and Child* looks all wrinkly because Leonardo may have mixed too much oil in the paint.

Detail of *Madonna and Child.* 1473. Tempera and oil on wood. Alte Pinakothek, Munich. Scala/Art Resource

Some things that happened to
Leonardo's paintings weren't his
fault. It seems that people just couldn't
keep their hands off his work.

The bottom of Ginevra de' Benci
(on page 12) was cut off, and part of the
painting of St. Jerome (page 14) was
cut in half and used as a tabletop!

Someone even cut the sides off

Mona Lisa. 1503.
Oil on wood.
Louvre, Paris.
Giraudon / Art Resource

Leonardo's most famous painting, the *Mona Lisa.*

Ever since Leonardo painted the *Mona Lisa,* people have been talking about the mysterious look the lady has—especially her smile.

No matter where you stand, the *Mona Lisa* is always looking right into your eyes.

Detail of *Mona Lisa*.

The background of the *Mona Lisa* is very interesting, too. It looks like it's part of a science fiction or fairy-tale world. In a strange way, *Mona Lisa* and the background seem to blend together.

St. John the Baptist. 1515.
Oil on wood.
Louvre, Paris. Scala / Art Resource

St. Anne, Virgin and Child.
1503. Oil on wood.
Louvre, Paris.
Scala / Art Resource

Leonardo painted only a few pictures after the *Mona Lisa*. He was more interested in working on his inventions and experiments. He spent the last years of his life in France, a guest of the King of France, making notes and drawings about his discoveries. He died there in 1519.

Leonardo da Vinci was one of the first artists to make his paintings seem real in all ways.

He gave the people in his paintings a feeling of movement and being alive.

He used dark shadows and light colors to make what he was painting seem to come toward you and away from the painting.

Detail of *The Virgin of the Rocks* on page 16

Leonardo made his beautiful backgrounds a special part of the whole picture.

He always tried to make his paintings as perfect and close to nature as possible.

Detail of *St. Anne, Virgin and Child* on page 29

Artists ever since Leonardo da Vinci have learned from the discoveries he made.

It's not easy to see a real Leonardo da Vinci painting. There's only one in the United States. The rest are in Europe.

The paintings in this book are in the museums listed below. Maybe some day you'll be lucky enough to go to one of these museums and see for yourself how beautiful Leonardo's work is.

Biblioteca Reale, Turin, Italy
Bibliothéque de Institut de France, Paris, France
Accademia, Venice, Italy
Uffizi, Florence, Italy
National Gallery of Art, Washington, D.C.
Hermitage Museum, St. Petersburg, Russia
Vatican Museum, Rome, Italy
Louvre, Paris, France
National Gallery, London, England
British Museum, London, England
Codex Atlanticus, Milan, Italy
Alte Pinakothek, Munich, Germany

LEARN MORE BY TAKING THE LEONARDO QUIZ!

(ANSWERS ON THE NEXT PAGE.)

1. Leonardo da Vinci was:
a Right-handed
b Left-handed
c Both

2. Some of Leonardo's favorite foods were:
a BBQ pulled-pork sandwiches with fries and cole slaw
b Minestrone soup, peas, white beans, salad, fruit, and bread
c Waffles with maple syrup

3. Leonardo was an excellent musician. What was one of his favorite instruments to play?
a A Les Paul Sunburst guitar
b An accordion
c A lyre

4. Which of the following are *not* Leonardo da Vinci inventions?
a The machine gun, a self-propelled cart, the parachute, and pontoon shoes for walking on water
b An underwater diving suit, a hang glider, and an armored tank
c Shoe laces, the windshield wiper, and spray cheese in a can

5. The *Mona Lisa* is displayed in the Louvre, a major art museum in Paris, France. How does the museum keep one of the world's most valuable and famous paintings protected from theft and vandalism?
a They release a pack of guard Chihuahuas each night after the museum closes.
b They apply sticky tar on the floor around the painting so security guards can follow the tracks of any would-be thieves.
c They keep the painting behind super-thick bullet-proof glass.

ANSWERS

1. c Leonardo was able to use both hands equally well. He could draw with one hand while writing notes (in reverse!) with the other. People who can use both hands easily are ambidextrous.

2. b Leonardo was really into nutrition and healthy eating. He seemed to prefer vegetarian dishes, such as white-bean soup, eggs, mushrooms, olives, salads, fruits, and bread. Some of his shopping lists did include beef, but the meat may have been purchased for his housekeepers and guests.

3. c Among other instruments, Leonardo was known to play the lyre, a U-shaped stringed instrument that's kind of like a small harp. He also invented the viola organista, a complicated instrument that was a combination of a harpsichord and a cello.

4. c Leonardo drew detailed designs for many modern-day inventions, including all of those listed in "a" and "b"! Hardly any of his designs were actually built during his lifetime, however. In most cases, the materials needed to construct Leonardo's inventions weren't available until hundreds of years later.

5. c The Louvre keeps the *Mona Lisa* in a sealed enclosure behind 1½-inch-thick bulletproof glass! It's also kept at the perfect temperature and humidity to preserve the paint and the wood panel surface Leonardo used for the painting.